T0070213

YONDER WONDERS

LIFE CHANGING REVELATIONS

ESSIE CROCKOM ROBERTS

authorHOUSE®

AuthorHouse™
1663 Liberty Drive
Bloomington, IN 47403
www.authorhouse.com
Phone: 1 (800) 839-8640

Published by AuthorHouse 08/31/2017

ISBN: 978-1-5462-0537-1 (sc)
ISBN: 978-1-5462-0536-4 (e)

Library of Congress Control Number: 2017912988

Print information available on the last page.

Any people depicted in stock imagery provided by Thinkstock are models, and such images are being used for illustrative purposes only. Certain stock imagery © Thinkstock.

This book is printed on acid-free paper.

Because of the dynamic nature of the Internet, any web addresses or links contained in this book may have changed since publication and may no longer be valid. The views expressed in this work are solely those of the author and do not necessarily reflect the views of the publisher, and the publisher hereby disclaims any responsibility for them.

Scripture quotations marked KJV are from the Holy Bible, King James Version (Authorized Version). First published in 1611. Quoted from the KJV Classic Reference Bible, Copyright © 1983 by The Zondervan Corporation.

Also by Essie Crockom Roberts
God's Reposition to Position

To those whose faith has been uprooted by neglecting time with the Father, who started out on a spiritual journey influenced by the Holy Spirit. They seemingly have not had any additional direction to continue the journey, I hope this book will help guide them on there way. To the depressed, lonely at heart, and those left behind—for the misused and the abused—trust God.

And Joshua said unto the people, Sanctify yourselves: for tomorrow the Lord will do WONDERS among you.

—Joshua 3:5

CONTENTS

INTRODUCTION

For whatever length of time you've been in a relationship with Jesus Christ, how does your present level of spiritual growth match up with the length of time you've known Him as your Lord and Savior? You must never retreat from your forward movement of life's spiritual growth in this earthly realm. Some days you may feel so close and intimate in your relationship with God, and other days you might feel totally out of touch with the spirit within. This can cause you to think you're in and out of the presence of the Holy Spirit, finding it difficult to permanently stay in His presence. God is always with you wherever you go: at home, work, school, a baseball game, or overseas. His spirit is inside you. You just have to continue to acknowledge it as such. He has sealed you and sent His Holy Spirit into your heart that you may know your sufficiency is from God.

> Whither shall I go from thy Spirit? Or whither shall I flee from thy presence? If I ascend up into heaven, thou *art* there: If I make my bed in hell, behold thou *art there*. If I take the wings of the morning, and dwell in the uttermost parts of the sea;

Even there shall thy hand lead me, and thy
right hand shall hold me. (Psalm 139:7–10)

For He has said, I will never leave thee, nor
forsake thee. (Hebrews 13:5)

One journey disappointment can make you stronger
for the next adventure in life. Allow it to be a learning tool
for the new project. We can learn much from our mistakes.
With Him there is no crisis mode for any problem, no
panic mode for any emergency. There's nothing God doesn't
know. He's already measured the earth, so there's not a place
you can explore that He doesn't know. There are absolutely
no detours around God. You must come in by the way
of His door, the door He has opened for you. His door
is our opportunity to be with Him, and we're safe with
Him. We are to live in His liberty and freedom, with the
understanding that the life we live is the sermon we preach
to those we come in contact with.

I am the door: by me if any man enter in,
he shall be saved, and shall go in and out,
and find pasture. (John 10:9)

Small-minded people can only build small things,
because they are small on the inside. There is nothing
comfortable with walking around with cramped toes from
wearing shoes that are too small for your feet. When growth
shows up, change comes on the scene. Growth speaks to
change. The shoes that fit your feet when you were five years

old cannot accommodate your feet at age twenty-five. Your feet demanded change.

Growth in God and His Word should bring about a change in the way you think and talk, your beliefs, how you treat others, and how you value the life He has given you.

Seasons change; they come and go. We cannot afford to remain in the same season all the while expecting to grow. Summer clothing will not adequately serve you in a cold winter season. We must be willing to let some things go and reach out to the newness that comes with the present of the Holy Spirit. We change and grow from season to season.

CHAPTER 1

A Place Where Utterance beyond the Power of Man to Put into Words Can Be Heard

In Acts 2, the Bible explains that on the day of Pentecost, there was a prayer meeting held in a place called the upper room. Jews dwelled in Jerusalem, and they were devout men. They came from every nation under heaven. As they gathered together, continuing to pray, the Holy Spirit appeared in such an unusual manner that everyone in the room was filled with the Holy Ghost. They all began to speak with other tongues as the Spirit gave them utterance. Something miraculous happened in that place. There was an utterance taking place, dispersed directly from the Holy Ghost.

> And they were all amazed and marveled, saying one to another, behold, are not all these which speak Galilaeans? And how hear we every man in our own tongue, wherein were born? (Acts 2:7–8)

1

This could be compared to an antenna with a directly radiating wave connection that enables you to hear in ways that you know only the Holy Spirit can convey a message, at which point you would know it to be true. It's impossible to articulate what the antenna was picking up, unless it's declared to someone with spiritual ability and an understanding of revelation to hear as the spirit reveals.

The Holy Spirit is a surveillance system; it detects and keeps watch. It's also a navigation system. It leads, guides, and gives close observation to the rhythm of the word. This is a harmonious movement, with all things working together for the good, one that directs to all truths. His truth is a shield and buckler for your protection. The rhythm has an exciting flow to it, so much so that it will allow you to dance with the Word, making sure you never miss a beat and that you remain in step all the way to the finish of the song.

It is so vast that it cannot be contained on the inside. There's always a surplus manifesting on the outside. It has the ability to spill over to the outside and make all that God has commanded to come to pass. This God kind of life is an empowered life, where enrichment becomes visible and never-ending, where you change the atmosphere with your very presence. It's where you operate on a different platform than most, in a different arena than most, and where you shift the atmosphere with the Word of God flowing from your mouth. Justice shows itself like a butterfly's unfolding wings, exposing and establishing righteousness in every dark corner of the world. It cannot be stopped. It cannot be influenced by negative input from others. The supernatural, intelligent power of God cannot be contained, just as wind cannot be contained in a fist or water be bound in a garment.

Now the Lord is that Spirit: and where
the Spirit of the Lord is, there is liberty.
(2 Corinthians 3:17)

How is it that God tells you to go to a particular place
when you don't know where the place is or how to get
there, nor do you have the means to get there? This now
becomes opportunity to trust in the Lord with all your
heart—not some of your heart, but all of your heart. Do not
dare to lean on any of your own understanding; it cannot be
trusted. Make sure to consult with and acknowledge Him in
every way, because He has a sure plan to direct you and get
you on your way to your designation. To know where your
help comes from is to understand that the results are there,
that they have already been established and opportunity is
waiting for you.

Using your own intellect and not having any regard or
consideration for the Holy Spirit can sometimes cause you
to make unwise decisions. Decisions have consequences that
can be good or bad, positive or negative. Every thought is
generated from a place, good or bad. Thoughts give the
imagination permission to form itself. Facts are not always
the truth; facts can sometimes lie to you, but God's word
can never be a lie. His truth stands unchangeable. You must
never allow your head to speak for your heart. Creation
begins from the inside, where the spirit of God resides,
where the overflow of the heart touches the mouth.

In Colossian 4, Paul asked the saints and brethren
in Christ to pray that God would open unto him and
Timothy a door of utterance to speak the mystery of
Christ, to speak a fresh, renewing word in the knowledge

of God to the saints so they'd be rooted and built up in Christ and established in the faith. As he spoke, he wanted the word to be clearly understood so there could be great manifestations among them.

When the God on the inside of you speaks and you don't understand what He's saying, it's because He's speaking to Himself inside you. You're not aware of all His abilities inside you in order to grasp what is being articulated through the Spirit. He's always orchestrating His creative power through His children. The Holly Spirit never sleeps.

You are the channel used to display the word. We may not fully realize how the remote control works, but it makes the connection. The channel cannot be clogged up by sin. There must be a cleared-away path for the connection to take place. We incapacitate ourselves when we do not deal with known sin in our lives. Sin makes us ineligible for the power of God to freely flow through us.

> *There* is no darkness, nor shadow of death, where the workers of iniquity may hide themselves. (Job 34:22)

CHAPTER 2

Why Did You Stop?

> And the Lord called unto Adam, and said
> unto him, where are thou? And he said,
> I heard thou voice in the garden, and I
> was afraid, because I was naked; and I hid
> myself. And He said, who told thee that
> thou was naked? Hast thou eaten of the
> tree, whereof I commanded thee that thou
> shouldest not eat? —Genesis 3:9–11

Adam disobeyed God and was deceived by another voice,
one that caused him to have shame. How did Adam know
the difference between being naked versus being clothed?
He listened to a voice that caused his curiosity to focus
outside the instructions of his Creator. God had commanded
him not to eat of the tree of knowledge, of good and evil.
But Adam did what God told him not to do, and then he
complained and shifted the blame to Eve. Eve blamed the
serpent. The two of them moved away from obedience into

disobedience, neglecting the command of God. It is never good to disobey God.

There was also a certain man in John 5:5–9 who had an infirmity, and for thirty-eight years he couldn't get help from anyone. He was impotent and couldn't help himself. This man believed he needed someone else's help to put him into a pool at the time the water was stirred up in order for him to receive appropriate healing.

> When Jesus saw him lie, and knew that he had been now a long time in that case, He said unto him, wilt thou be made whole? The impotent man answered Him, Sir, I have no man, when the water is troubled, to put me into the pool: but while I am coming, another steppeth down before me. Jesus said unto him, rise, take up thy bed and walk. And immediately the man was made whole, and took up his bed, and walked: and on the same day was the Sabbath. (John 5:6–9)

The man had excuses as to why he accepted his condition for so long. He couldn't see beyond his present state. His mind was filled with, *I can't do this. I can't do that. I can't move my legs. I can't walk.* He was familiar with defeat only. He spoke defeat, saying, "I have no one to put me into the pool," looking to others for assistance.

He felt sorry for himself. He was addressing questions Jesus had not asked him. His focus was on complaining, making excuses, and blaming others. The attention was on the problem rather than the problem solver.

Jesus simply asked, "Wilt thou be made whole? Rise, take up thy bed, and walk."

In other words: Get up; don't sleep in that condition one more night. Take up your bed and remove it from the ground, the low place. You carry the bed; do not allow the bed to carry you any longer.

You will not be able to return to that unproductive place of stagnation, failing to progress, being motionless, always procrastinating, never advancing, never having development toward growth or purpose. He didn't have a spiritual voice speaking to his forward progress. At that point his restoration was beyond him.

The children of Israel continued looking backward, complaining all the way—so much so that they missed seeing the blessing. Don't let God's momentum skip past you and miss your day of visitation. Look, see God, and get the help you need now.

> I will lift up mine eyes unto the hills, from whence cometh my help. My help *cometh* from the Lord, which made heaven and earth. (Psalm 121:1–2)

Rise up and walk. Rise above blame, above shame, and pay no attention to finger pointing. Begin to think of yourself differently, and you will be able to live differently. See your situation in the light of your desires, and your mind will begin to make the shift. You will notice a change beginning to take form in your situation, empowering and motivating you to the absolute truth of God, thereby establishing and taking responsibility for truth. The best way to recognize error is to know the truth.

Consider the following four questions:

1. Why did you give up?

If you've been given a word from God, where He has pointed you in a particular direction, with the leading of His Spirit, you must then take the initiative to begin the journey toward what you believe He's said. After stepping out, you might think, *Am I doing it right?* and consider pulling back. Don't worry if you make a step in the wrong direction. God has the power mixed with grace to get you back on track. Don't feel like a failure to the point where you quit. If in fact He gave you the ability to hear Him once, you can hear Him again. If He has not said anything new or different, then it is still what He said at first. Don't quit, because you'll never get there if you stop. Why have a wound if you cannot show what caused the wound? Don't take a journey or even a walk for no reason. Take it with purpose in mind. Make it count for something. Accomplishment is on the other side of the journey. When others said you couldn't, God said you could, and being diligent is a sure way to accomplish gain. Forsake the foolish things and foolish people; live and go in the way with His instructions before you.

> I can do all things through Christ which strengtheneth me. (Philippians 4:13)

2. What pulled you away from purpose, putting destiny on pause?

Sometimes being preoccupied with life's daily challenges—the job, office, business, money problems, friends, and so much more—can be a huge distraction, which can cause us to neglect our relationship with the Father. The real purpose in life gets pushed to the back burner. Sometimes the burner gets turned all the way off; there's no heat being generated. The Word is no longer active. Influence gets filtered in from other sources not connected to the purpose and will of the Father. The focus shifts to whatever environment we associate with that is dominating our lives. It can sometimes be that very shifting that pulls your focus from purpose. Dependence then falls on whatever cause the distraction..

Hunger and thirst must be for God. There's nothing designed to ever take the place of God's plans for your life on His earth. God's instructions must be the driving force in the life He has created for you to rein in and have dominion over.

Enough! You have put up with the enemy's framework and plots in opposition against you long enough. Go with what God says, and allow what He says to happen in all life's circumstances.

> "For I know the thoughts that I think toward you, saith the Lord, thoughts of peace, and not of evil, to give you an expected end. Then shall ye call upon me, and ye shall go and pray unto me, and I will hearken unto you" (Jeremiah 29:11–12).

3.   What or who caused you to fall short of finishing the race you were supposed to win?

It was predestinate for you to finish in victory with a big win. To obtain the victory, one must stay in the race. There is a key designed especially for you, made to unlock your dream door that's nesting inside you, ready to make a move and manifest itself. There are things trapped inside you, waiting for you to declare them, ready to take flight. The spirit word on the inside of you is so much greater than the world on the outside. Do not take your eternal rest with your dreams locked inside you, void of understanding that the race is not given to the swift or to the strong but to those who endure to the end. You were running the race well. Who hindered you that you didn't obey the truth? The fact is you were already a winner, and that's the truth. You're a force to be reckoned with. If you're facing a mountain, you must began to move that mountain, if need be—take it down one shovel at a time. Keep digging, keep moving, and keep going. Don't look down but keep looking up. God can take down the mountain and can lift up the valley by putting you on a plain level.

> Nay, in all these things we are more than conquerors through Him that loved us. (Romans 8:37)

> Wherefore seeing we also are compassed about with so great a cloud of witnesses, let us lay aside every weight, and the sin which doth so easily beset us, and let us run with patience the race that is set before us. (Hebrews 12:1)

4. Why are you allowing others to set the pace for your life?

Do not allow loyalty to friends or other relationships keep you from moving forward, or let some self-inflected wound cause you to get weak along the way. Sometime others are not willing to go in the same direction as you. You must stop trying to take people to places they don't want to go. Don't be caught by the hunter going about seeking whom he can devour. From henceforth let no man trouble you, for why do you allow your liberty to be judged by another man's conscience or to be controlled by others? Let the peace of God invade your life. Whenever you doubt, don't turn away from God but instead turn to Him. Be not affected by human bias and criticism. Do not be intimidated or threatened by any person or group of people. The box they created for you cannot hold you. Small-minded people can only build small boxes. They are too small to hold you captive or keep you confined within walls they constructed for you. Your completeness, your fullness, everything necessary for you to rein is in Christ. Circumstances do not dictate to God what He can or cannot do. There's nothing too hard for Him to do nor nothing too easy that He will overlook. He does not have to pause to take a breath. He faints not, nor gets weary.

Walking and talking with God are two essential steps to maintain a healthy relationship with Him. Try increasing your vocabulary based on the Word of God. Condition your mind by using the spoken Word, which has creative power. Shift your language—change the way you talk from negative to positive. Regain your Holy Ghost consciousness. The responsibility is yours to keep yourself in the presence of

Christ the Lord. When was the last time you renewed your thinking (mind) with the Word of God?

Allow Him to give you true quietness and be still. When God gives quietness, who then can make trouble?

> A man shall be satisfied with good, by the fruit of his mouth….. (Proverbs 12:14)

> Beware lest any man spoil you through philosophy and vain deceit, after the tradition of men, after the rudiments of the world, and not after Christ. (Colossian 2:8)

CHAPTER 3

Carry Your Cross; He Will Deliver You and Your Cross

No more excuses. You have too much in front of you to allow your focus to linger and tarry, looking behind you and delaying your future blessings. Whatever is in the rear, you've passed already. Dragging the past along in life will contaminate your future. There is no life behind you; life is ahead. Aim and press forward.

> Brethren, I count not myself to have apprehended: but this one thing I do, forgetting those things which are behind, and reaching forth unto those things which are before, I press toward the mark for the price of the high calling of God in Christ Jesus. (Philippians 3:13–14)

You will never get where you need to be until you reframe from going back to where you used to be. Continue doing what He said to you at first, until He says something new.

Application is vital, so apply the Word you know. Knowledge is power. The just is delivered through knowledge. Lack of knowledge can cause one to become confused and eventually get destroyed by the works of the enemy. To believe is great, but to know is profound. The Lord did not say He believed the thoughts He thinks toward you. What He said was, "I know the thoughts that I think toward you." He already knows the outcome of every situation that troubles you, even your smallest concerns.

He will most likely reveal what He will bring you to, before He reveals what He will take you through in order to get you to where He is taking you. You will be protected even in the wilderness, and your dry experience will turn into a green, watered garden.

> Faithful is He that calleth you, who also will do it. (1 Thessalonians 5:24)

> Therefore I say unto you, take no thought for your life, what ye shall eat, or what ye shall drink; nor yet for your body, what ye shall put on. Is not the life more than meat, and the body than raiment? Behold the fowls of the air: for they sow not, neither do they reap, nor gather into barns; yet your heavenly Father feedeth them. Are ye not much better than they? (Matthew 6:25–26)

God did not bring you this point in life to leave you. He weighted the load before it was given to you and made sure you had the ability to carry the load. A master plan was put into place for your escape. Take all that's been given to you by God, use every tool, and build Him a house. Everything you need for construction has been created by the Father. Life can be a whirlpool of living or it can be a still, watered, green-pasture experience. Do not let your hand become slack when doing God's work. Live with nothing to hide, without sin in your closet.

You can never do too much for the kingdom. Allow your cup to run over. There will always be someone there to catch the overflow, as it was when Jesus took two fishes and five loaves of bread and lifted them up to heaven, blessed them, and then gave them to His disciples to serve a multitude of people. There were about five thousand men who did eat and were filled, not including the women and children, yet twelve baskets full of food remained.

> Oh Lord our God, all this store that we have prepared to build thee an house for thine holy name *cometh* of thine hand, and *is* all thine own. (1 Chronicles 29:16)

CHAPTER 4

Draw from Deep Wells

Wells, in this case, are an indication of God being the source of our salvation.

> Behold, God is my salvation; I will trust, and not be afraid: for the Lord JEHOVAH is my strength and *my* song; He also is become my salvation. Therefore with joy shall ye draw water out of the wells of salvation. (Isaiah 12:2–3)

Jesus is an everlasting well, the source of true light, as the Samaria woman, who went to Jacob's well one day to draw water, found out.

> "Now Jacob's well was there. Jesus therefore, being wearied with his journey, sat thus on the well: and it was about the sixth hour. There cometh a woman of Samaria to draw water: Jesus saith unto her. Give me to drink" (John 4:6–7).

Then saith the women of Samaria unto Him, how is it that thou, being a Jew, askest drink of me, which am a woman of Samaria? For the Jews have no dealings with the Samaritans. Jesus answered and said unto her, if thou knewest the gift of God, and who it is that saith to the, give me to drink; thou wouldest have asked of him, and he would have given thee living water. The woman saith to him, Sir, thou hast nothing to draw with, and the well is deep: from whence then hast thou that living water? Art thou greater than our father Jacob, which gave us the well, and drank thereof himself, and his children, and his cattle? Jesus answered and said unto her, whosoever drinketh of this water shall thirst again: but whosoever drinketh of the water that I shall give him shall never thirst; but the water that I shall give him shall be in him a well of water springing up into everlasting life. The woman saith unto him, Sir, give me this water, that I thirst not, neither come hither to draw. (John 4:9–15)

The woman saith unto Him. I know that Messias cometh which is called Christ: when he is come, he will tell us all things. Jesus saith unto her, I that speak unto thee am he. (John 4: 25-26)

Coming to the conclusion and understanding that Jesus was not speaking of the water that the physical well embodied, the woman dropped her water bucket and went on her way to tell the others what had happen to her at the well, the encounter she'd had with Jesus. The broken pieces of her life had been restored to wholeness. She didn't realize that she was empty inside. It wasn't drinking that she had need of, it was the fulfillment of what was missing in her life. Her soul was dry and thirsty for the Living Water (Jesus Christ). She had tried to fill her emptiness with people and was merely existing, having artificial fulfillment only. She'd had five failed marriages and was in a relationship with a man who did not belong to her.

Relationships with others can never be totally satisfying until our relationship with God is in its proper place. Momentary pleasure cannot sustain a lifetime of fulfillment, which only God can provide.

> The woman then left her waterpot, and
> went her way into the city, and saith to the
> men, come, see a man, which told me all
> things that ever I did: is not this the Christ?
> Then they went out of the city, and came
> unto him. (John 4:28–30)

Jesus refers to the water that He gives as having everlasting life, continuous and ageless. His well is always full; in Him dwells all fullness.

How do you draw the maximum from a full well? You do so with an empty vessel. God's living water has absolutely no side effects, because it was designed to give us the abundant life that only He can offer.

God always increases us from the inside to the outside. The well holds the water on the inside. Take not your vessel to the well, expecting to draw water from a leak on the outside of its walls. The water is inside the well, so go deep to gain the maximum.

When you fill up the gas tank of your car, it will carry you for many miles, as opposed to only putting in a few gallons. A few gallons will give you only a few miles of travel. A full tank will give you many miles of sightseeing pleasure before having to stop for refueling. The same applies when we fill our spirit to the maximum that it can hold daily, perhaps not perceiving what we may or may not unexpectedly encounter. Every time we engage in the Word of God, whether in prayer, in praise, in worship or just spending time with our Lord, we get refilled and energized, able to move forward without concerns of running out of or running low on spiritual fuel.

The deeper the well, the deeper the drawing vessel must travel to reach the top of the water lever. Water is held in reserve so that it can be drawn as needed, but if the drawing vessel is not secure enough, meaning the vessel could possibly contain some small holes that leak or a handle that is not secure, then there will be no capacity to retain the water. The question then becomes, what is the value of the holding vessel? We are vessels created to be used.

Drawing from shallow wells can be problematic. They often run dry in hot summer months when water is most needed for vegetation, or when one is most thirsty from the heat, needing to be refreshed often. Shallow wells can also suggest that one would have to travel deeper downward to the water level in order to draw from the low-level well.

Why hang around wells that are without water, broken cisterns that cannot hold water, or people who do not have a relationship nor the desire to have a relationship with the Father?

> For my people have committed two evils;
> they have forsaken me the fountain of
> living waters, and hewed them out cisterns,
> broken cisterns, that can hold no water.
> (Jeremiah 2:13)

It is to our advantage to search for the deep wells in relationships that we feel are necessary in life. Keeping continuous company with nonbelievers or even lukewarm believers can sometimes bring about distractions and cause one to have an uncommitted relationship with the Father. A polluted well falls into the same category as a dried-up well—neither can function or be of the service for which it was intended.

> The earth which drinketh in the rain that
> cometh oft upon it, and bringeth forth
> herbs meet for them by whom it is dressed,
> receiveth blessing from God. (Hebrews 6:7)

Once in a dream, I saw a large flesh wound, and the wound was deep and red inside. As the dream progressed, I looked into the wound and observed a small pin–sized head beginning to form a healing pattern at its depth. It was healing from the inside out, and complete healing was taking place.

The revelation from that dream was this: whatever is broken in your life and making an appearance on the outside, the repairing must began from within. Speak the Word. Digest the word. Cover the wound with the Word of God.

Drop your water bucket.

There is a well inside you, so there's no need for the water bucket anymore. You were once broken but now restored from that broken place. You're healed and renewed, and God made it possible. God breathed into your nostrils, so you just have to continue to draw from His source of life, Jesus Christ.

Deep calleth unto deep…. (Psalm 42:7).

Get beyond your own understanding, and extend yourself far beyond the surface. This will never be understood with the natural mind but only by the spiritual intellect. Sometimes we just have to be filtered by God. There will perhaps come a time when you will have to excuse yourself from the presence of dysfunctional saints. You just have to walk away from some things and some people. Dysfunctional believers operate in what I call the spirit of piggybacking. They won't take the time to acquaint themselves with any personal knowledge of God or anything else, for that matter. They depend on you or others to gain spiritual knowledge and afterward totally depend on you to give them a piggyback ride all the way to the Promised Land.

> Counsel in the heart of a man is *like* deep water; but a man of understanding will draw it out. (Proverbs 20:5)

The deepest well that can be drawn from is God and His Word. As a dry sponge soaks up liquids, we must allow our spirit to soak up the spirit of God and His Word. The Word is a faith adjuster, always progressive. It will remain and continue to live as we abide in it and continue to draw from it as our main source, freely giving it out as it was freely given to us. Intake determines output.

Through knowledge shall the just be delivered.

In Luke 10:39–42, we see Mary sitting at Jesus's feet, listening to His word. Her sister, Martha, was caught up in doing much serving and preparation work. Perhaps Martha could have believed Mary was taking the easy road or just being lazy.

Martha then complained to Jesus, saying, "Lord, dost thou not care that my sister hath left me to serve alone?" She was likely thinking *There's so much to do, but Mary's just sitting there looking up at you. Why isn't she helping me serve?*

Jesus at that time set Martha straight, saying, "Martha, Martha, thou are careful and troubled about many things: but one thing is needful: and Mary hat chosen that good part, which shall not be taken away from her."

Mary had her attention focused on Jesus.

There is no need to worry if you have given your life totally to Jesus.

Take a launch out into the deep and receive fresh manna daily from the Word of God. You have this one and only life to live. Live it to the fullest. Why cast away such a precious life that was freely given to you in exchange to live beneath the awesome privilege of a loving Father, who has freely given you all things?

There was never a design for you to live low and down under the sins of the world. You are to live above, not beneath; you are the head, not the tail. Christ is your source, His supply, of which you are the beneficiary, designated to receive all that belongs to Him, is endless.

Gather from what you have planted and from what you have labored for. If you have not sown anything, what is there for you to harvest? The seed you sow is the seed you will reap. The zucchini is sometimes hiding behind the leaves or in the thick of the stalks.

Sometimes God wants us to search out a matter before we make the decision to move forward so ignorance doesn't become a party to our decision. It can cause us to lean on our own understanding, but we must always trust God in His way of doing things. He will exalt us when we humble ourselves before Him. We must learn to develop an appetite for what is good, where the entire meal is centered around the main course, desiring the meat of the word. Do not come to the dinner table looking to sit in a high chair, expecting milk and cereal to fill you up. Come to the dinner table with an expectation of receiving a fully balanced meal. Come boldly before the throne of grace.

For every one that useth milk *is* unskillful in the word of righteousness: for he is a babe. But strong meat belonged to them that are of full age….. (Hebrews 5:13–14)

CHAPTER 5

Light Shines Its Brightest in Darkness

For God, who commanded the light to shine out of darkness, hath shined in our hearts, to *give* the light of knowledge of the glory of God in the face of Jesus Christ. But we have this treasure in earthen vessels, that the excellency of the power may be of God, and not of us. —2 Corinthians 4:6–7

You were designed to be a light in the world, to live in a lighthouse, traveling with the light, forever shining, always mobile and willing to enter into dark corners of the world, applying the brightest of all light. The outcome of spiritual blindness is separation from the almighty God. You are to help unify, mobilize, care for, and open the eyes of the blind, turning them from darkness to the perfect light of Jesus Christ our Lord and Savior (ref. Acts 26:18).

How much of heaven's light will you allow to manifest or to be recognized through you in a dim and dark world?

Could it be as much as a candle that brightens a small section, or maybe a flashlight to target a certain area? Could it be as a table lamp that illuminates and brightens a room? There is a porch light to lighten the darkness around your home, or a streetlight to give illumination to all who travel on their way.

The abundance that comes with God's blessing is designed to cast the glorious shadow of His light on all who may be around you at any given time, be it one second or one year. Light is designed to expose and remove darkness. You're the only one who can give darkness permission to cast a shadow over the light within you. Your character will speak about you before you open your mouth. Cast the illumination of your spiritual knowledge and target your light on a dark place.

> Ye are the light of the world. A city that is set on a hill cannot be hid. Neither do men light a candle, and put under a bushel, but on a candlestick; and it giveth light unto all that is in the house. Let your light so shine before men, that they may see your good works, and glorify your Father which is in heaven. (Matthew 5:14–16)

Light shines its brightest in darkness. If light is absent, then darkness is present. It's impossible for light and darkness to occupy the same space. It's difficult to retain that which cannot be contained. Keep the light shining and the darkness will disappear. It's inconsistent for our light to shine bright one day and the next day be left on the countertop unused. Hot one day, cold the next day. Once the light is turned off, darkness automatically appears. Most darkness is just unformed purpose. Stay in the light and stay with the light. Jesus Christ is the light of the world.

In Matthew 25:1–13, the Bible tells of ten virgins of whom the kingdom of heaven is likened to, who took their lamps (lights) and went out to meet the bridegroom. Five virgins were wise and five were foolish. The five who were foolish did not use wisdom, not thinking their lamps could possibly run out of oil before the bridegroom would make his arrival. They didn't take extra vessels of oil to replenish their lamps in case of shortage.

Would it be wise to go on a long distance, say on a three-month camping trip, taking a flashlight without extra batteries? What good is the flashlight without batteries? The five wise virgins took extra oil for emergency purposes in case they ran out. Sure enough, the bridegroom was late in coming, and they all fell asleep while waiting.

At midnight there was a cry announcing the bridegroom's arrival and that it was time to meet him. They all rose and trimmed their lamps. The five foolish virgins were out of oil; their lamps had gone out during the night. They asked the five wise virgins if they would give them some of their oil. They had not brought extra, so the five wise virgins couldn't or wouldn't accommodate them.

The suggestion was made to the five foolish virgins to go purchase oil for themselves. Unfortunately, while they went on their journey to purchase oil, the bridegroom came; they who were wise went in with him to the marriage. When the marriage began the door was then shut tight. The five foolish virgins returned from purchasing oil, but it was too late to enter. They were in a bit of panic mode, shouting and beating on the closed door. Lord, Lord open the door to us. He answered saying, "verily I say unto, I know you not."

> Watch therefore, for ye know neither the
> day nor the hour wherein the Son of man
> cometh. (Matthew 25:13)

We must keep our lamps filled with the oil of the Word of God, burning bright at all times, so that at whatever hour the Lord appears, we will be ready to receive Him. Preparation for His coming cannot be deferred to the last minute. When the light is out, darkness appears; if one is without light walking in darkness, he or she becomes unrecognizable.

> Yea are all the children of light, and the
> children of the day: We are not of the night,
> nor of darkness. (1 Thessalonians 5:5)

Spiritual light is essential. It will always be recognized. It's developed from within. Darkness does not understand light and is most comfortable in the company of those who live and walk in darkness. When darkness sees you approaching, it runs in another direction because it's afraid of the light. Light will also change the effectiveness of darkness.

The only communication light has with darkness is to recognize it and then say to it, "We're not alike; we're from two different sources, so come over to the light." What fellowship hath righteousness with unrighteousness and what communion hath light with darkness? The answer is none.

> In Him was life and the life was the light of men. And the light shineth in darkness: and the darkness comprehend it not. (John 1:4–5)

Live in the light. When you're the light shining in a dark place, others will be drawn to you by the brightness. Look no more on the outside; it's formed within. Embrace what's already on the inside—it's the Spirit of God, and you must allow it to manifest itself outwardly. The light of the Lord can penetrate all the illusions concocted by the enemy, which is designed to orchestrate and lead you onto the wrong path, keeping you off the course that will achieve your God-given purpose in your life on earth.

God wants the oil of heaven to be flaming, burning its brightest, that all the world may see and know Christ within you.

> The way of the wicked *is* as the darkness: they know not at what they stumble. (Proverbs 4:19)

> Let your light so shine before men, that they may see your good works, and glorify your Father which is in heaven. (Matthew 5:16)

> The entrance of thy words giveth light; It giveth understanding unto the simple. (Psalm 119:130)

Thy word *is* a lamp unto my feet, and a light unto my path. (Psalm 119:105)

Light came into existence by God speaking the very word itself.

In the beginning God created the heaven and the earth. And the earth was without form, and void*; and* darkness was upon the face of the deep. And the Spirit of God moved upon the face of the waters. And God said, Let there be light; and there was light. And God saw the light, that it was good: and God divided the light from the darkness. (Genesis 1:1–3)

The Lord *is* my light and my salvation; whom shall I fear? The Lord *is* the strength of my life: of whom shall I be afraid? (Psalm 27:1)

This then is the message which we have heard of Him, and declare unto you, that God is light, and in Him is no darkness at all. If we say that we have fellowship with Him, and walk in darkness, we lie, and do not the truth: But if we walk in the light, as He is in the light, we have fellowship one with another, and the blood of Jesus Christ His Son cleanseth us from all sin. (1 John 1:5–7)

CHAPTER 6

A Yonder Calling

Wisdom sometime is deferrable, meaning it is withheld for an appointed time in the future, when needed. Jesus explained this concept in the book of Luke 24:49: "And behold, I send the promise of my Father upon you: but tarry ye in the city of Jerusalem, until ye be endued with power from on high."

He wanted the disciples to linger in expectation and wait on a particular supernatural power orchestrated from on high by the Holy Spirit, with the full weight of His glory upon it.

A yonder calling can be seen in this same light. The word *yonder* means an indicated distance, space, or time in view. It can be seen from afar—something approaching, getting closer and closer as you continue to move toward what you see in the distance. It's that space between where you are and where you desire to be. The capacity to reach it can be subjected to adversity, misfortune, or even affliction. Sometimes it's an uphill climb, other times a down-in-the-valley experience, or a maybe a blinding blizzard, but if you have the faith to hover over what you're seeing in the distance, rest assured you and God's promise to you will make the appropriate contact.

Wonders, meaning something new to one's experience far beyond anything previously known or anticipated, come with the amazing and the astonishing leading of the Holy Spirit, so captivating you will know that it is for you. Somehow you know it's good, and you can see it before you make actual contact with it. You can discern it in the Spirit before it manifests. There's an exuberant excitement when you can see something new and different on the horizon, especially with the glory of the Lord attached to it.

In olden days, particularly in southern states, a phase such as "yonder they come" was used, indicating the person who was expected could be seen from a distance.

How do we apply this concept to a spiritual visualization? Jesus is always moving toward His children, and at the same time we should be moving toward Him with great anticipation of someday seeing Him face-to-face. Everywhere we go, the wonder-working Savior is there, working wonders on our behalf, with spiritual discernment we must be able to recognize His approaching. The destination is set, and it's the actual journey that can consume the greatest amount of time. When time is involved, we must remain focused, desiring godly results and seeing it happen by faith in Him. Your blessing can come out of your adversities. Adversity is a special soil for generating miracles. If adversity is present in your life, your miracle is knocking at your door.

> But as it is written, eye hath not seen,
> nor ear heard, neither have entered into
> the heart of man, the things which God

hath prepared for them that love Him, but God hath revealed *them* unto us by His Spirit: for the Spirit searcheth all things, yea, the deep things of God. For what man knoweth the things of a man, save the spirit of man which is in him? Even so the things of God knoweth no man, but the Spirit of God. Now we have received, not the spirit of the world, but the spirit which is of God; that we might know the things that are freely given to us of God. Which things also we speak, not in the words which man's wisdom teacheth, but which the Holy Ghost teacheth; comparing spiritual things with spiritual. But the natural man receiveth not the things of the Spirit of God: for they are foolishness unto him: neither can he *know them,* because they are spiritually discerned. (1 Corinthians 2:9–14)

In my first book, *God's Reposition to Position*, I was instructed by God to put pen to paper and tell of a real-life experience the Holy Spirit had guided me through. It being my first book, I was inexperienced in putting it together, and as a result I made some mistakes, which I regret. But no mistakes in the message were articulated. The message was facts and truth. There were two friends in particular who read the book only for their own judgmental purposes, and they were so judgmental that they missed the real message of the book—so much so that they contacted me by phone not to congratulate but to criticize. What helped me through that moment was that I knew I had been instructed by the Holy Spirit, and He had a plan for the book, mistakes and all. I also knew it was the Holy Spirit who had initiated the gift within me. God is committed to completing whatever He initiates.

Some months later, one of those friends was confronted with a serious problem of her own, which she thought had no solution, and became troubled at heart. The problem forced her to go back and read the very book she had criticized, searching for an answer to resolve her situation. This time she didn't criticize but searched for answers in hope of finding how to get through the pain. After reading the book again, she was able to get clarity in order to dig herself out of a deep pit.

God uses imperfect people to convey a flawless message in order to get an accurate point across to His people. Do not reject God using you because of your flaws or imperfections. Remember, He is the Perfect One. You just need to say *yes*!

WHO IS HE

Alpha and Omega,
Beginning and end,
First and last,
The Father,
The Son,
The Holy Spirit.
Savior,
A wonder,
Son of God, Son of Man,
The Savior of the world.
Emmanuel, (God with us,)
Lamb of God,
Redeemer,
Lord of all creation.
Lord of Lords,
King of Kings,
Jehovah,
Creator,
Comforter,
Master,
Good Shepherd,
All-powerful God,

Giver of Life,
Light of the world,
Bright and Morning Star.
The Way, the Truth, the Life,
Wonderful.
Counselor,
Mighty God,
Prince of Peace.
Love,
The Highest Authority,
And He is coming again.

"SONGS FROM MY HEART"

1

<u>There is a river.</u>

There is a river.
There is a river.
There is a river.
A peaceful river, flowing from my heart,
Refined for God's glory,
Chosen in the furnace of affliction.
Purified and holy,
make me, Lord,
for your glory.
There is a river;
You healed my body,
Saved my soul,
Comforted me, and
You made me whole.
There is a river.

#2

Comfort me, oh Lord.

Comfort me, oh Lord.
You are the comforter of my soul.
Come, oh Jesus, come, oh Lord.
You are the comforter of my soul.
Teach me, and I shall know,
Lead me, and I shall go.
Comfort me, oh Lord.
Be a miracle unto me.
Hold my hand.
Guide my feet.
Keep my tongue
As I follow thee,
And be a miracle unto me.

#3

Still Comes

Lord, you see me.
Lord, you hear me.
Lord, you know me.
And you love me *still*.
Still come the morning,
solid as the night,
glowing in the sun,
shining oh so bright.
Morning began the next day,
Even in the blackness of the sky
or darkness of the day.
Whether you are in it or not,

Still it comes.
Happy or sad, it comes,
Rich or poor, it comes,
Rain or shine, it comes,
Still!

CONTACT THE AUTHOR

Email: essrob@comcast.net
Web: www.essiecrockomrob.com

P.O. Box 630722
Littleton, CO 80163-0722

ABOUT THE AUTHOR

Born in Shreveport, Louisiana, Essie Crockom Roberts began serving the Lord at the tender age of eleven. She relocated to Pasadena, California, in her teen years and attended Pasadena City College and Cypress College Cypress ,in California. She later attended the School of Design Methods in Hollywood, California, to study engineering and electrical design. She spent more than twenty-eight years in electrical engineering.

Her ministry is that of a call to testify about the gospel of grace of God wherever she goes. She tells of her faith, how it doesn't stand in the wisdom of men but in the power of God. She studied, promoted, and participated in street evangelism for many years. Having never been blessed with biological children, God turned it into something good by blessing her with an abundance of spiritually blessed born-again children.

She is the founder of A Place of Worship Ministries in Littleton, Colorado. This is her second book. *God's Reposition to Position* was published in 2014.

ABOUT THE BOOK

Reading *Yonder Wonders* will help you polish your life with the newness and freshness of the Holy Spirit within you.

This book was written under the leadership and guidance of the Holy Spirit. It will inspire the reader not to stop on his or her way to purpose or give up on the call of God. This book will encourage the believer to keep an open ear to the voice of the Spirit of the Lord because it will lead you to all truths.

Believe in bigger and better things. Gather new visions, create new goals, and dream greater dreams. The dream on the inside wants to connected to the outside, to become a reality and manifest itself.

Every experience you've had in life was once a present choice. Seeking God will always cause you to make right choices in life. But even if you make wrong decisions, continuing to seek God will lead you to the paths He's carved distinctly for you. You're just a few steps away so remain focused. Never give up on your belief in God. Stay strong in the Lord.

Printed in the United States
By Bookmasters